Succeed
With Me

To my sister, Yvette, who has left me her energy.

Succeed With Me

Life's little positive thinking book

Selwa Anthony

NEW
HOLLAND

Published in Australia by
New Holland Publishers (Australia) Pty Ltd
Sydney • Auckland • London • Cape Town

14 Aquatic Drive Frenchs Forest NSW 2086 Australia
218 Lake Road Northcote Auckland New Zealand
86 Edgware Road London W2 2EA United Kingdom
80 McKenzie Street Cape Town 8001 South Africa

First published by Pan Macmillan Publishers Australia in 1993
Reprinted by Pan Macmillan Publishers Australia 1993, 1994
This edition published by New Holland Publishers (Australia)
Pty Ltd in 2004

10 9 8 7 6 5 4 3 2 1

National Library of Australia Cataloguing-in-Publication Data:

Anthony, Selwa.
Succeed with me.

ISBN 1 74110 159 X.

1. Success - Psychological aspects. 2. Optimism. I. Title.

158.1

Publishing Manager: Robynne Millward
Editor: Liz Hardy
Printed in Australia by McPherson's Printing Group, Victoria

This book was typeset in Aldine 721 BT 12pt

Foreword

Selwa Anthony is the wisest woman I know.
Whatever she has to say about succeeding is well
worth studying.

Dr Colleen McCullough

About the Author

Selwa Anthony was born in Cowra, NSW, the fourth child of a family of seven, to her Lebanese-born parents, Abraham and Josephine Anthony. Proud Australians, they always instilled in their children how lucky they were to be born in this wonderful country and Selwa was introduced to Australian writers at a very early age. So proud was her father that he would introduce his children as his 'seven little Australians' (after Ethel Turner's book, which became one of Selwa's favourites).

Before starting her own literary agency in 1985, Selwa worked in retail, first in fashion then in bookselling. From the mid-seventies Selwa managed a major chain of bookshops until her friend, Colleen McCullough, encouraged her to become a literary agent. Selwa is now one of Australia's leading literary agents, running a very successful author management agency with over sixty published Australian authors. She has also established Australian Voices In Print

(AVIP), an association for promoting Australian publications.

As a bookseller, Selwa had noticed a gap in the market for Australian popular fiction and, since then, has pioneered the new breed of popular fiction authors in Australia (the late Evan Green was her first popular fiction success). Her agency now covers all areas of Australian publishing. In 2001, she successfully launched the first ever Popular Writers' and Readers' Festival in conjunction with the NSW Writers' Centre, now an annual event.

Selwa's success, both personal and professional, is due to her great belief in positive thinking. Selwa is married with two daughters and a stepson and stepdaughter.

Acknowledgments

My special thanks to Jimmy Thomson for making this book possible. He was able to put my exact thoughts down on paper. For this I am eternally grateful.

Thank you to my husband Brian Dennis and my daughters Anthea and Linda for always believing in me.

Heartfelt thanks to the following people for your generosity in allowing me use your wonderful inspirational thoughts: Mary Coustas, Eden Gaha, Scott Gibbons, Maggie Hamilton, Toni Lamond, Sandra Lee, Jeanne Little, Mark Macleod, Tara Moss, Guzin Najim, Father Chris Riley, AJ Rochester, Terry Underwood, Sorrel Wilby and Lynne Wilding.

Thank you to project editor, Liz Hardy, for her gentle touch and my assistant, Selena Hanet-Hutchins, for her keen eye and being my angel.

Contents

Preface

It's been over ten years since the first publication of *Succeed With Me* and I have been delighted with its ongoing success.

I was inspired to write this little book by a very negative event that took place in my life in 1992. My dear sister, Yvette Clarke, died from cancer, leaving this world with so much of her life still to be lived. Throughout my life I have always been able to turn a negative into a positive, up until this particular challenge.

For some weeks after her death I was very angry and found myself thinking more negatively than I have ever done in my life. That was until my inner voice took over, telling me there has to be something positive. I immediately began to search for exactly that.

At the time, my eldest daughter, Anthea, was in a musical group performing in clubs throughout New South Wales. As busy as my own authors' agency was, I was also managing the group, sometimes being out three to four evenings a week. Then it struck me: where was I getting this extra energy? How was I able to run my very busy authors' agency, dealing with each author on a personal basis, and still have the time to manage and motivate this young musical group? Then I understood: it was my sister Yvette's energy. She had energy to burn and she had passed it on to me to continue using it to the best of my ability. This was the positive that came from her untimely death. Another part of the energy she left me went into a success seminar and awards night that I started in November of 1992, for my authors, friends and publishers. These 'Succeed With Me' seminars, dedicated to the spirit of my sister, have continued ever since, with full attendance every year.

The main thrust of 'Succeed With Me' is directed at the *Me* in your life—at yourself. But all the self-improvement is geared towards a much wider idea.

I believe that once you have begun to sort yourself out—and certainly not before—you should then use your new-found power, energy and confidence as part of that network.

Friends, family and colleagues will, in a very natural and gradual way, become part of that network. New people will be drawn in. Others may drift away. But the end result will find you at the centre of a network, which feeds off your strength, then feeds back more than you have given. And everybody benefits. 'Succeed With Me' is a fine example of simple networking. Successful, positive people, joining with other successful, positive people. Nobody succeeds in this world alone. Success, whether it be in business, friendship, or relationships, depends on the giving of positive energies to each other.

Very recently, I found myself experiencing panic attacks, deep depression and loss of appetite. I couldn't believe this was happening to me. Until then I thought I was a superwoman, but now I had an opportunity to practise what I'd preached, proving no-one goes it alone. I wasn't too proud to seek help from my family, friends and colleagues, letting them know I needed all their positive energies around me while I worked through those dark days. I can't stress enough how important it was for me to be surrounded by those positive people and have the support of their positive energies.

An example of networking on a business level, which indirectly led to the writing of the original *Succeed With Me* book, is the story of how I met Jimmy Thomson.

His wife, journalist (and now a dear friend) Sue Williams, had been sent to Norfolk Island to interview the author Colleen McCullough. While there, Sue mentioned that her husband wanted to move out of journalism into books. Colleen, being a friend of mine, suggested he should get in touch with me when he had a project in mind.

Back in Sydney, award-winning cartoonist, Eric Löbbecke, a friend of Sue's, asked if she'd be interested in writing a children's book for him to illustrate. She said no, but she knew someone who would be—Jimmy.

Jimmy brought the book to me and, to cut a long story short, *The Koala Who Bounced* was published in 1993 by Random House, with many reprints since. From that initial contact, I now represent not only that brilliant artist and author team, but Sue Williams as well.

The book *Succeed With Me* is, itself, an example of how I work my success and it will show you how 'Succeed With Me' will work for you.

To clear things up for you the reader, the *Me* in 'Succeed With Me' is *you*. This book will show you—in the simplest possible way—how to succeed in every area of your life. It will show you how to use your positive energy when you are surrounded by negative energy.

I am not showing you anything that I have not already tested on myself. Everything in this book is possible. When you get *Me* right, it creates a positive energy that will draw people to you.

The quality that makes this different from every other self-help book—and makes it uniquely Australian—is its down-to-earth practicality. It is not full of easy answers—there are none. This is a book written for ordinary people, to show how you can become extraordinary … if you want to.

Of course, life doesn't always run smoothly—there are often obstacles put in our way. But don't let that prevent you from staying positive. My advice is to stop and take a deep breath, pick up this little book and find a way to move around the barriers.

Always remember the people who helped you along the way—so you in turn can do the same—once again pointing out the basis of 'Succeed With Me'.

Here's to every success!

Selwa Anthony

How to Remember All You Read in This Book

Have you ever heard a piece of music and been transported back to a time, a place and a person you'd almost forgotten? The memories are so strong you can almost smell the air and taste the food.

That power of words, sounds or smells is a potent aid to your memory for everyday use and not just nostalgia.

At the end of each chapter, you will be given a symbol. You should use that symbol, an ordinary object, to anchor the lessons of the chapter in your mind.

Thereafter, whenever you see that symbol or even hear it mentioned, it will act as a trigger and you should remember the lessons you learnt in that chapter.

And before long, every day, as you go about your normal routine, the messages in this book will come flooding back to you like memories of old friends.

Try it. It works.

*Thanks to Roger Anthony for his Triggers and Anchors system from his motivational seminars 'Crocodiles Not Waterlilies'.

Chapter 1

What Does 'Succeed With Me' Mean?

It's a simple idea, based on positive thinking and focused on you as the centre of a 'success network'.

First you get the *Me* part right by following a six-step success plan.

Then you become the kind of person with whom people want to share success. In effect, you become the one saying 'Succeed With Me'.

Getting *Me* right involves six initial steps:

• Liking yourself
• Believing in yourself
• Trusting yourself
• Being generous to yourself
• Challenging yourself
• Testing yourself.

Then there is the final principle: sharing success.

In Chapter 8 we'll look at how to put those first six ideas into action as the focus of a success network.

A success network is a group of people like you who want to succeed and want to share their efforts—and success—with others.

I'll explain why you are more likely to succeed when you share your success.

As well as those six principles, the word SUCCEED will guide everything we do. This is how it works:

S is for Self-confidence

This is the essence of 'Succeed With Me': using positive thinking to like yourself, believe in yourself and trust yourself. You must master those three principles before proceeding any further.

You are the most important person in your world—accept that and build on it.

U is for Understanding

Know where you're going and where you're coming from. Ask what the motivations are that drive you and those around you.

It's not just knowing how—the trick is knowing why.

C is for Creativity

Curiosity, ambition and imagination are what lead to progress. Expand your horizons—break free from the routine.

If it's okay to do the same old things every day, maybe you shouldn't be doing them at all.

C is also for Collaboration

Why go it alone? Working together makes it easier and the success is more satisfying.

Success on your own is just another form of failure.

E is for Excellence

Always do everything as well as you possibly can. Always push for that glimpse of perfection.

'Good enough' is no good at all.

E is also for Enjoyment

Learn to enjoy what you do, enjoy your success, and enjoy what your success brings.

Successes are people who are paid well for doing something they'd gladly do for nothing.

D is for Determination

Set your goals and keep heading straight for them.

Problems are opportunities waiting to be exploited. Obstacles are stepping stones. Mountains are there to be climbed.

But you have to be prepared to work hard to reach your goals.

If it doesn't hurt a little, you're probably not trying hard enough.

These SUCCEED ideas will be discussed in greater detail in our Power Pages.

Finally, there are a number of Smart Thinking tips scattered through the book to help you use positive thinking in everyday situations.

People who sneer at positive thinking haven't tried it. You're not only going to try it, you're going to learn how to apply it.

If 'Think Positive' sounds dumb to you, take a look at the alternative.

With that in mind, turn to Chapter 2 and start to learn to like yourself.

Every time you see a plus sign or a cross, or read about one or hear one mentioned, remember the power of positive thinking.

Power Page 1

Positive Thinking— The Power to Change Your Life

Two runners in a marathon are neck and neck only a mile from the finish.

One of them thinks, 'I'm not going to make it. All my strength is gone. My rival looks too strong …'

The other thinks, 'It hurts but I can handle it. I know I have something left. Besides, my rival looks beaten …'

Who's going to finish first?

This is the power of positive thinking.

It means:

• Changing your attitude can change your life.

• Believing you will succeed makes success more likely.

• You can be a better person just by wanting to.

Maybe life wasn't meant to be easy—but you can make it easier.

It takes just as much energy to think negatively as it does to think positively. But thinking positively gives you strength rather than draining you.

Smart Thinking

Don't Get Mad—Get On With It!

When someone does something to hurt you, don't get mad, don't get even—just get on with it.

Revenge is rarely sweet. It's often stupid and it's never the end of the story.

Looking for revenge is just looking for trouble.

If someone goes out of their way to upset you, the best form of revenge is to say and do nothing. That takes up none of your valuable time or energy.

Why try to get even when you can be getting ahead?

Never act in anger. Wait until your rage subsides—however long it takes—then decide what you *want* to do. If you're really hurt, write a letter saying why in as much detail as you can manage. Then throw it away. You've got it off your chest, so let it go.

Remember the second E from SUCCEED: Enjoy. Enjoy your life, don't poison it with bitterness and frustration.

You can't ignore problems. But you can decide *when* and *how* to deal with them.

When is when you have had time to think coolly and rationally—not when you feel like lashing out.

How is acting in a way that leaves no doubt about what you want, without any sense of aggression or retaliation.

And while you're pondering what to do and when and how to do it, think positively about what has happened.

If someone has hurt or harmed you, was what happened deliberate or just careless?

If someone has let you down, was it because they wanted to or because they couldn't help it?

What's more important: to tell someone they were wrong or to tell them you are angry?

Is it better to have someone as a friend or an enemy?

It's easier to lose friends and create enemies than the other way round.

'My mother always wrote in our autograph books, "not failure, but low ambition is a crime", and that's why I've always accepted an opportunity without fear—if you fail at something you can always try again, but if you lack confidence and say no, you'll always regret not having tried.'

Jeanne Little, entertainer and
Australian icon

Chapter 2
Learning to Like Yourself

It's a strange idea, isn't it? That you have to like yourself—and that you might even need to learn how to do it.

Maybe you are quite happy with the kind of person you are and the image you present to the world.

If so, good for you! But you should read this chapter anyway. It will help you understand what you're doing right and you might get some new ideas.

If you can't honestly say, 'I like myself', or if you are not sure, this chapter is vital. Ask yourself this:

If I don't like myself, how can I expect anyone else to like me?

When you like yourself, you are able to say, 'I wish I had someone like me as a friend.'

So how do you learn to like yourself more?

It's all about feeling good about yourself, which starts with feeling good about the way you look.

Feel good—look good

The two are intertwined. Change one and you can change the other.

Start with the way you look, if only because that's the easiest way to break your cycle of failure.

Remember how you feel when you've just had your hair cut, or just bought new clothes that suit you perfectly? You should feel that good every day.

If you look miserable, you'll get sympathy.
If you look positive, you'll get support.

Even when you are down, make yourself look your best and people will respond to your positive image.

In turn their positive reaction will lift your spirits. So by looking your best you will end up feeling better.

Your appearance tells people how you feel about yourself, so don't shackle yourself to a drab exterior.

You can't judge a book by its cover—but how else can you tell if you want to read it?

The first thing to do is go and look in a mirror. Make a list of all the things you don't like about your appearance.

Now go through them one by one and make the best of what you've got.

Have your hair done, buy new specs or switch to contact lenses, get your teeth fixed, trim your beard, improve your make-up—every little improvement helps.

Remember D is for *Determination*. You have to work at this as if it is a mega-budget project. After all, you want to end up looking a million dollars.

Just by trying, you are already succeeding. Doing nothing is the greatest failure.

Buy or borrow a copy of a book called *Colour Me Beautiful* (there's an edition for men too) or call one of the agencies listed under Image & Colour Consultants in the *Yellow Pages*.

To put it simply, the books or the consultants will tell you what colours you should be wearing, using your natural skin tones as a guide.

When you wear the right colours, you come alive. When you know what colours to wear, you never waste your money on 'wrong' clothes and you always look your best.

It may only be a scarf or, for men, a tie, but the difference it makes is astonishing. Don't knock it. It works.

Once you've discovered which are the best colours for you, revamp your wardrobe. Many large department stores have fashion consultants who will help you. You don't have to change your whole wardrobe at once. Just wearing the right-coloured scarf or tie can make the world of difference.

Each small step is an improvement. Every time you buy an item of clothing, make sure it is the right colour. Do as a friend did and dye older clothes to the right shade.

Every day you should look in the mirror and like what you see a little more.

Now take a good long look at yourself. Do you think you're too fat or too thin? Do you feel sluggish and tired?

To be at your best you need to eat well and to exercise. There's no need to join a health club or become a gym junkie. Walking, swimming or cycling will do just as well.

Try getting off the bus or train a stop or two from your workplace, or park your car further away. That walk in the morning and at night will make all the difference.

There's no need to go on a crazy crash diet. All you need to do is use a little commonsense.

You only get one body—look after it and it will last a lifetime!

Eat less fatty foods and more fresh fruit and vegetables. It's that easy. When you start eating better you'll feel brighter, stronger and healthier.

You will be in better shape too.

Every step you take makes the next step easier.

A friend was very down, both physically and emotionally, until she went to see a colour consultant. Wham! She realised that part of her problem was that she was trapping herself in the wrong colours.

She changed her wardrobe, even her hair colour, and looked and felt much better. She was then inspired to start losing weight.

This woman was a dietitian. She knew better than most about healthy eating, but she had been so miserable that she had become a junk food junkie.

But now that she'd broken the vicious cycle by making herself look good, she felt good and didn't want to eat rubbish any more. The better she felt the better it got. And that's what will happen to you.

As you change, and appreciate the power you have to change yourself, your confidence will grow. You will look good. You will feel good. Everything will begin to get better.

Every time you see a mirror, or read about one or hear one mentioned, remember how important it is to like yourself.

Succeeding With Others

If you like yourself, others will be more inclined to like you.

Friends who once felt sorry for you will now feel admiration and envy.

By being positive and liking yourself, you will be more likely to choose friends who are positive.

Liking yourself gives you the confidence to make new friends and business contacts on *your* terms.

Personal and work relationships will thrive as you lose the need for constant reassurance.

People will respect your judgment more, especially when you disagree with them, because they will know you are not driven by the need to boost your ego.

Succeed With Me

'Every single "no" gets me a step closer to a "yes".'
Eden Gaha, producer and presenter

40

Power Page 2

S is for Self-confidence

Success starts with self-confidence. Without that, you're going nowhere.

And the wonderful thing about success and self-confidence is that they feed off each other.

Recognise each small success in your life and your confidence will grow.

Use that confidence every time you attempt something and your chances of success will increase.

It works. And the more it works the easier it is.

Self-confidence makes the possible probable.

You can do anything you truly want to do. We're not talking about impossible dreams— just realistic achievable goals.

Go just one step further than you've ever gone before and your confidence will blossom.

When you can do what you want, why would you want to do anything else?

Smart Thinking

Don't Expect Everyone to Like You

Life is a lot of things, but—unless you are a politician or a movie star—it is not a popularity contest.

Even then, as the great actress, Bette Davis once said, 'If everybody likes you, you're not doing it right.'

That doesn't mean you should go out of your way to be disliked—there will always be people who will dislike you, regardless of what you do or say.

People who have struggled to succeed might find your seemingly effortless success hard to swallow.

People who have given up on their own lives might find your success rubs salt in their wounds and reminds them of their own failures.

Some people simply don't like anybody.

But that's their problem. If people set out to dislike you, leave them to it. What harm can they do?

But if you try to make them like you, you'll be frustrated and diverted from your goals.

Liking yourself is enough—and it gives you at least one true friend for life.

Chapter 3
Believing in Yourself

Now that you're starting to like yourself, you have to start believing in yourself.

It's all a question of *positive thinking*.

Believe in your ability to change your life.

Positive thinking works because the happier and more confident you are, the more likely you are to succeed. Then, when you do succeed, you feel even happier and even more confident, and so on.

When you're feeling down the answer is to pick yourself up, not to try to get used to it.

I am constantly telling my family to turn negatives into positives but I was put to the test when my sister Yvette died after losing a long battle with cancer.

One of my daughters challenged me on this saying, 'How can you find anything positive from Aunt Yvette's death? She had so much to live for and so many who loved her. She didn't deserve to die.'

I have to admit that I was stumped for a while. Yvette was such a source of strength for me; I found it hard to reconcile my insistence on thinking positively with my deep sense of loss and despair.

But something amazing was already starting to happen. A pain I had been suffering in my shoulder—just where Yvette had her cancer—disappeared overnight.

Furthermore, once I knew she was no longer suffering, I felt as if a load had been lifted from my shoulders and been replaced by a surge of energy.

Then I realised what was happening.

I had lost Yvette but her energy was still there. In fact, I decided I would take it on, just as I might don one of her favourite cardigans. So, despite the fact that I was already overburdened with work, I began a number of projects—I moved into new areas that I'd never tackled before and tried harder than ever.

And instead of feeling more tired and more stressed, I felt stronger and calmer than I'd ever been. I felt Yvette's energy flood through me.

I tell this story to show that, no matter what, negative thinking is just a waste of time and energy. You must learn to turn negatives into positives.

In day-to-day living, a bad day at work might be the impetus you need to find another, better job.

A bout of ill health might give you time to take stock and provide the determination you need to get yourself fit.

A major disappointment may be the trigger you need to examine what you want and what you need from life.

The further down you go the more 'up' there is to aim for.

And remember C and E from SUCCEED: *Creativity* and *Enjoyment*.

When things go wrong, be creative and find a way to turn them round. Treat it as a game and enjoy the challenge of turning negative into positive.

Then you can enjoy life when it starts to go right again.

Negative thoughts have negative results. And

even if you do get lucky and things turn out okay, you'll be too gloomy to enjoy it.

Believe in your ability to make yourself feel good. When you feel good, tell yourself:

'I want to feel like this every day—and I will.'

Recall that feeling whenever you get down—it's a reminder that life can and does get better. Think positively! *Believe* that you are a worthwhile person.

To improve your positive attitude, spend more time with people you like and who like you. Spend as little time as possible with negative people:

- People who are always complaining the world is against them
- People who like to show how clever they are by putting others down—including you
- People who are always criticising others behind their backs, especially mutual friends

- People who always find fault with the world, whether it's waiters or coworkers, the weather or the wine list.

Give them a wide berth.

Believe in the creative rather then the destructive.

For some reason, we are attracted to things that horrify and terrify, disturb and disgust us. For the time being, you have to cut them out.

If you see or read something that upsets you, and you *can't* do anything about it, steer clear of that kind of material. The TV news has enough horror for anyone to cope with. But leave the video nasties to the ghouls.

By all means confront the bad things that you *can* do something about. Give to charity. Join a pressure group. Write to your MP. But only when you are strong enough.

Change your own life before you start trying to change the world.

Believe in the people closest to you.

Get in touch with the people you care about

and, in particular, spend more time with those you love.

In a period of change, you will still need some reassurance. Don't ask the cynics: that's just asking to be put down.

Go to the people most likely to give you strength when you need it. Let them know if you are hurting. Talk your problems through. Listen to their advice, even though you will eventually make your own decision about what to do.

Talking things through with others can help put your problems into perspective. Take the opportunity to make others feel part of your success.

Remember C is for *Collaborate*.

Tell one very close friend exactly what you are doing. Tell them about this book and the advice it gives. Invite them to help you and to monitor your progress. They will be honest, and that means telling you when they see an improvement.

Believing in yourself means believing in others too.

In the meantime, at some point you're going to have to examine your attitudes and discover where you've been going wrong. This is the U from SUCCEED.

U is for *Understanding*.

Understand your mistakes, but don't dwell on them. And don't be too tough on yourself.

Remember this:

You are never as wrong as you think you might be.

Believe in your ability to learn from your mistakes and live with them.

If things do go wrong, say you're sorry, fix what you can, then get on with your life. No one can ask any more of you.

Mistakes are made in the past ... success is in the future.

From now on everything gets better.

Check out books that help to give you a positive attitude. And say this to yourself every morning:

'Today I will do my best to be better than I've ever been.'

Try, and already you're starting to succeed.

Every time you see an aeroplane, or read about one, or hear one mentioned, remember how important it is to believe in yourself.

'Believe in yourself when no-one else does—it will carry you through to ultimate success.'
Lynne Wilding, author

Succeeding With Others

Believe in yourself and others will believe in you.

Positive people are drawn to others who have a strong belief in themselves.

Negative people, once they realise they can't pull you down, soon leave you alone—or may even start to become positive themselves.

The ability to believe in yourself makes you better able to believe in others.

You will soon find yourself at the centre of a network of people who believe in themselves, believe in each other and believe in you. That network will be the basis of your mutual success: growing and changing but always strong.

'We've got to have the courage to demand greatness from our young people. They will always surprise us with their clear-sighted vision, their determination, their generosity, their capacity for love and their eagerness to be loved.'

Father Chris Riley, founder of the charity Youth Off The Streets

Power Page 3

U is for Understanding

To have confidence in yourself, to believe in yourself and to trust yourself—the three key elements of 'Succeed With Me'—you have to understand yourself.

Ask yourself why you want to succeed. Why do you feel you are not a success? What does 'success' mean to you?

To know where you are going, you must know where you started from and understand what has brought you this far.

Ask yourself why you are doing some of the things you do.

If they're part of your overall plan, or to help someone in your network, or simply something you want to do—that's good.

But if you're doing things because you feel guilty, because you're scared to say 'no', or you can't think of anything better to do—that's bad.

If you're doing things for the wrong reasons you're not in control of your life.

None of your past mistakes matter, but if you understand why you made them you'll be less likely to repeat them.

Learn from the past and put it behind you—look to the future and grasp it with both hands.

Smart Thinking

Don't Fight Others' Battles

When you are full of self-confidence and flushed with success, there is a natural tendency to want to take on the world.

When you come across someone who feels they're getting a raw deal, there's an urge to play the knight in shining armour.

Don't.

If people ask you for advice, give it freely and sincerely. But don't take it as an invitation to invade their lives and solve their problems.

People often ask for advice without any intention of acting on it. What they are doing is using you as a sounding board before making up their own minds.

Give advice and moral support but leave it at that unless you are asked to do more.

And even then be very careful.

Remember the U from SUCCEED: *Understand* what people really want from you.

When you teach a baby to walk, there is a time when you have to hold them and a point at which you have to let go.

When people are learning to fly planes, there's a time when they are always accompanied by an instructor, and a point at which they have to fly solo.

When you're helping someone, there's a point at which holding them up becomes holding them back.

Recognise the point at which you have to let go.

Don't go down with the drowning man. Even lifesavers put self-preservation first.

Some people become addicted to others' strength. They ask for help, they get it, and so they go on asking. Your strength is like a drug to these people. You give time and energy—they give nothing but trouble.

They are draining you and you're not really helping them.

Take away the drug. Make them go cold turkey. People *need* the chance to stand up for themselves. So don't rush to be a knight in shining armour.

Everyone has the right to slay their own dragons.

'Live life. Really live it. The only true failure is the failure to give it a go.'
Tara Moss, model and author

Chapter 4
Trusting Yourself

You like yourself, you believe in yourself; now you have to trust yourself.

Aren't trusting yourself and believing in yourself the same thing?

No—at least not for the purposes of this program.

In fact, there is a simple, practical distinction.

You can believe in yourself or anyone or anything without putting yourself or them to the test. But it's trust that you need when you do test yourself.

To put it another way: believing is thinking, trusting is doing. Belief is thought, trust is action.

You may believe a ladder would hold your weight, but it's only when you start climbing that you trust it.

That's what I mean by trust. And that's why trusting yourself is the next step to positive action. If you can't trust yourself, who *can* you trust? The trouble is, a lot of people don't trust themselves—and they don't trust anyone else either.

Even so, too often we allow our lives to be ruled by what other people want us to do.

Can we blame others if their priorities are different from ours? Should we be surprised if their goals are never exactly the same as ours?

Have we then any right to feel cheated or disappointed when life doesn't turn out the way we had hoped?

We trust other people when we don't even trust ourselves because it gives us someone to blame when things go wrong.

Trusting yourself is just a question of overcoming your fear of failure. Notice I say *overcoming*—not *eliminating*.

Fear is good. It is one of the strongest emotions we are born with and we are foolish to try to fight it. Successes use their fear. It gives them an edge.

TV and stage performers, sportsmen and women, politicians and business people all over the world testify to the fact that fear is what pushes them to give their very best.

Fear also makes you stop and think about what you are doing.

Fear is a reminder that things *can* go wrong, not a premonition that things *will* go wrong.

Recognise your fears and use them. Use them to check whether you are sure about what you are doing. Use them to sharpen up your performance.

The brave confront their fears. Only the foolhardy ignore them.

Trusting in yourself is all about confronting your fears. It is saying, 'I may be wrong, but I believe I'm right, so I'm going to do this my way.'

Trusting yourself is also saying, 'If I turn out to be wrong, I trust my ability to handle whatever happens.'

Trusting yourself turns desire and ability into results.

It's all about trusting your judgment and taking chances.

You take a chance every time you cross a road. Chances are you'll get to the other side.

You take a chance every time you travel by plane. Chances are, you'll reach your destination.

You don't get anywhere without taking chances.

But you look both ways before you cross the road. You don't book with a dodgy airline. Then you go.

Trusting yourself makes you a more interesting person.

Look around you. The world is full of steady, dependable people going nowhere. *Successes are risk takers* and risk takers trust themselves to get it right.

What's more, other successes—good bosses, for instance—admire people who trust themselves. They are more likely to trust you. They are probably risk takers too, after all.

Trusting yourself means taking control. It is your most public expression of positive thinking.

It means that when your ideas are at least as good as those suggested by others, you say, 'Let's do it my way.'

If you're going to succeed, succeed at your own plans and you can take full credit. If you're going to fail, at least fail trying your own ideas.

Trusting yourself means *always* doing your best.

When you go out on a limb to do what you believe is right, it's your reputation that's at stake, so you will automatically give it your very best shot. Whenever you give your best, the chances of success are so much greater.

Trusting yourself means doing what others only talk about.

How often do you hear people say, 'I could have done that' when someone else makes a success of something—anything from a business to a book?

Could have—but didn't.

Why? Because, even though they may have had the same brilliant idea, they didn't trust themselves to see it through and they didn't trust their own judgment. They didn't take the risk.

Their fear of failure was greater than their belief in themselves or their bright idea.

They did nothing because that was easier. They didn't enjoy success because they didn't deserve it.

They didn't trust themselves.

Trusting yourself uses so many elements from SUCCEED.

The *Self-confidence* to take a chance.

The *Understanding* to recognise the pitfalls.

The *Creativity* of new ideas and getting things to go right after they begin to go wrong.

The *Enjoyment* of getting a result by doing things your way.

The *Excellence* that can only be achieved by taking risks.

The *Determination* to give your ideas the best possible chance to succeed.

Every time you see a traffic light, or read about one, or hear one mentioned, remember how important it is to trust yourself.

Succeeding With Others

Recognise others' genuine fears and don't dismiss them out of hand. That way, they will trust you more. And they may have a point.

When you begin to trust yourself you will find that people instinctively start to trust you more.

They will be drawn to your positive attitude.

They will be attracted by the mere fact that you are more interesting.

They will want you to trust them and they will want to prove themselves worthy of your trust.

You will find yourself better able to tell who you can trust and who you can't.

People who can't be trusted will shy away from you because of your positive attitude.

'My hope now is for people to live peacefully together in love ... Without love we can do nothing.'

Guzin Najim (from *The Promise*, by
Sandra Lee, the story of Guzin
Najim's escape from Iraq)

Power Page 4

C is for Creativity

As a matter of course you are called upon at work to use your skill, your experience and your knowledge.

But anybody else doing the same job might have these qualities.

What you bring to any job or project is your imagination, your instinct and your flair.

In a word: *Creativity*.

It is a myth that only some people are born creative. Everyone is born with the capacity to at least *become* creative in some way. But you have to find your creativity and channel it into your work.

Creativity is a way of putting your personality into your work. It puts your signature on everything you do.

Using your creativity gives you back something worth more than a weekly wage. It gives you pride and confidence.

Anybody can be creative at work but you have to work at being creative.

Find your creative talent and find a way of using it—even if it means looking for another job.

Smart Thinking

Obstacles—and Why They Exist

Recognising that there are obstacles in life is not negative thinking. It's commonsense.

Sometimes something, or someone, gets in the way of your plans. And if you can't get past, or go over it, the answer may be to go around.

Before you can build a bridge you must get to the other side of the river.

So don't keep banging on a door if no-one wants to open it. Find a window, or a way around the side of the house.

Remember the first C from SUCCEED: be *Creative*.

If at first you don't succeed, try again—then try something else.

Giving up is not giving in—it's just a question of conserving your energy.

And don't forget, obstacles may be there to tell you that you're going in the wrong direction.

Consider that carefully before you try to go any further.

Chapter 5
Be Generous With Yourself

Being generous with yourself is one of the hardest of the six steps to take. When we are not as successful as we would like to be, we tend to punish ourselves.

But, as any teacher, psychologist or successful businessperson will tell you, reward is a much more effective motivational tool than punishment.

That applies as much, if not more so, to you.

Reward yourself for trying, and you'll want to try harder. Punish yourself and you'll fear failure so much that you'll never try anything.

Don't forget, you are the most important person in your life.

If you can't make life good for yourself, you have no hope of helping make it better for others.

Be generous with your praise.

Appreciate the hard work you've done. At the end of each working day, make a note of your 'failures' so you can put them right the next day.

Then remember your successes. Allow yourself to feel good about doing things well.

If you're your own strongest critic, then your praise is worth savouring.

Be generous at home.

Your home is your haven from the cares of the day—don't allow it to be the source of more stress.

Make sure that there is one room that is *your* room. Even if you share it with a partner, make it clear that there will be times when you *must* be left alone.

Buy a 'Do Not Disturb' sign and make sure everyone knows it means what it says.

Make sure everyone in your home does their fair share of the domestic duties. Running around after everyone else makes them lazy and you get taken for granted. Make others appreciate the work you do by getting them to do their bit.

You can't be in control at work if you're a slave at home.

Be generous with your time.

Allow yourself the time to do things properly. Don't take on more than you can reasonably handle just to show how willing you are. Enthusiasm is appreciated but results are rewarded. Give yourself the time you need to complete each task properly.

Better late than never, better never than no good.

Allow yourself the time to read, relax and enjoy yourself. Reading and relaxation are food for the mind. Don't starve yourself.

Be generous with your money.

It's good to give others gifts, and it's good to give some to yourself, too. Remember that the greatest gift you can give those who care about you is for them to see you happy, successful and fulfilled.

You work hard for your rewards—so reward yourself. That new business suit or outfit is more important to you than the latest style of designer clothes is to your child.

That weekend away—alone or with your partner—is more important than an expensive 'duty' dinner with people you don't care about.

Pay the debts you owe yourself first: let everyone else wait in line.

Take the woman who had to set up home on her own with her two young daughters. She took a flat opposite their school and gave lodgings to a student who, in exchange for the accommodation, looked after the two girls while the woman was at work.

She took two jobs so she could afford a newer unit in a more pleasant environment, rather than a cheaper, drab unit that would have been depressing. But when her friends came to visit her they were shocked.

'You've kept the biggest and best room in the house for yourself,' they complained. 'You've got the best furniture and even the TV. What about your daughters?'

'My daughters are happy. They have everything they want,' she replied. 'I have two jobs but every minute I can, I spend with them. They are well-educated, well-fed, well-clothed and, most importantly, well-loved.

'However, when I'm on my own, I want to be able to relax as much as I can. I need to recharge my batteries. I need to feel secure. If I didn't have this room I wouldn't be able to hold down two jobs and they wouldn't have a home at all.'

That woman was a success then and she is a success now.

Every time you see a diamond, or read about one, or hear one mentioned, remember how important it is to be generous to yourself.

Succeeding With Others

When you've learned to praise yourself, you'll know how much others appreciate being praised by you.

When you've tried rewarding rather than punishing yourself, you'll know it will work with others.

When people know how much you value your time they'll be grateful for the time you spend with them.

Time is your most valuable gift—give it generously but wisely. Giving people gifts or money is a one-way transaction. Give them time and they will repay you with interest.

When people see you are prepared to look after yourself they will believe you are capable of looking after them. Prove that once and their loyalty will be yours forever.

'I love the Buddhist words "When the student is ready, the teacher appears." That teacher is often the person I least expect—the boss who makes life difficult; the one child in the family who doesn't seem to "get it". When I was younger I wasn't always ready to learn from them, but most days now I am.'

Mark Macleod, publisher

Power Page 5

C is for Collaboration

Throughout this book I describe ways you can succeed with others. The final chapter is about sharing your success.

There is little point in striving for success if you are not prepared to share both the burdens and the rewards.

Being self-confident and independent doesn't mean isolating yourself. Someone who is truly independent has the courage to take control when necessary, and to take orders, too.

Working *with* people is better than working *for* them or *against* them. It's also much better than working alone. Establish a success network and no one in it will want to see you fail.

Share your goals, divide your load, and multiply your successes.

Solo voyagers are lonely heroes.

'When someone throws a spanner in the works, just remember what a useful tool a spanner is.'
Sorrel Wilby, television presenter
and author

Smart Thinking

Taking 'No' for an Answer

It doesn't matter how positive you are, or even how right you are, sooner or later someone in a position of authority will say 'no' to you. Your demands will be dismissed. Your fears will be rejected.

It may be because they're no good.

It may be because the other person is in a bad mood.

It may be because the other person wants to prove they have power over you.

Whatever the case, you should speak up. Make sure you explain your point of view as clearly as possible. When you've done that, get on with what you have to do.

Remember the S from SUCCEED: your *Self-confidence* should be strong enough to allow you to back down without feeling that you've failed. And that makes the disagreement less of a personal conflict.

By speaking your mind, but avoiding con-
frontation, you have presented a solution rather
than a problem.

**It's better to be known as a problem
solver than a troublemaker.**

Chapter 6
Challenge Yourself

By now, if you're putting what you've learned in this book into practice, life should be a bit easier.

You may be achieving the same for less effort.

Or more for the same effort.

Both of these results miss the point. You should be able to achieve a lot more for a little more effort.

Remember the first E from SUCCEED? E is for *Excellence*.

Nobody's perfect—so there's always room for improvement.

You should aim for what you want to do, not what you've always done or think you can do.

Just by trying to do better, you *will* do better— even if you don't achieve what you set out to do at first.

Aim high and you'll shoot high. Aim low and there's nowhere else to go.

Challenge yourself to achieve more.

If you have been doing a certain task in a certain way for a long time, try to do it better, or get it done sooner, or do more in the same time.

The level at which you work well on a regular basis is not your upper limit—it's your *lower* limit.

You may not be able to do it easily, but you can always do it better.

Challenge yourself to enjoy your work more.

That's the other E from SUCCEED—*Enjoy*. Ask yourself if you're getting enough out of what you do. Maybe if you made your work more demanding, you'd find it more rewarding and more enjoyable.

You have to actively enjoy as much of your work as you can. If you're merely contented, you're not really trying.

If you get pleasure from a job well done, what do you get from a job done better?

Challenge yourself to grow.

If you trust yourself and believe in yourself, you *need* more responsibility to thrive. You must accept new challenges gladly or you'll never grow.

You learn from challenges and get confidence just from accepting them. When you succeed, your confidence grows.

'Knowing your limits' is just accepting defeat—reaching your limits must be your goal.

Challenge yourself to be positive.

Positive thinking is the basis of everything in this book. For the book to work for you, you have to think positively whenever you can.

When you are feeling down, depressed or disappointed, challenge yourself to find a way up.

Remember the first C from SUCCEED? C is for *Creative*.

The bigger the problem and the bigger the challenge, the greater the rewards in meeting it.

There is success in just accepting a challenge—the only certain losers are those who walk away.

Every time you see a ladder, or read about one, or hear one mentioned, remember how important it is to challenge yourself.

'Life is an intricate and beautiful dance of possibilities. We can stick to our notions of how we believe things should turn out, or we can allow life to unfold before us gently and profoundly, so that we're always in the right place at the right time.'

Maggie Hamilton, author

Succeeding With Others

When people see that you are prepared to set yourself challenges, they will be glad to be set challenges by you.

Challenging others brings out the best in them. Not challenging them encourages them to give up.

Tell people the challenges you've set yourself. They will admire your ambition and praise your achievement. They will also keep you honest.

When positive people know the challenges you've set yourself, they will help and become part of meeting those challenges—and part of your success.

When others realise that you relish challenges, they will offer you new ones and will respect you and reward you when you accept them.

'There is no right or wrong track—it is one track called life. If you just keep going then there is no such thing as failure.'

AJ Rochester, author, presenter and performer

Power Page 6

E is for Excellence

Excellence is not about being better than someone else.

Excellence is about being the best you possibly can be.

Someone you see as a rival may have lower standards and less potential than you have. Why be limited by their horizons?

Competing with others is sport—competing with yourself is a true test.

Excellence is not about being the best at what you do, it's about being better than you've been before.

As you surpass your own standards, you may find you *are* the best. That's good—provided you keep trying to be even better.

Try to excel at your work, in your personal relationships and in your leisure activities.

Work harder, not necessarily longer hours, at your job. Make sure the time you spend at home isn't wasted—be there for those who need you. Play harder too, even if it just means walking that extra mile.

Excellence *is* success. Being less than your best is being a failure.

Smart Thinking
Taking Control Without Giving Offence

Imagine you are a passenger in a car on a long journey and the person driving isn't doing a good job. You know you can drive better and could complete the journey more safely and possibly faster.

But no one accepts being told they are a bad driver, so what do you do?

You could ask the driver to do you a favour. Say that you've never driven that model of car before and you'd like to try.

You could offer to do the driver a favour. Say that they must be tired, or they're missing the scenery, and they should let someone else share the driving.

There are many ways you can take control without giving offence, even in a sensitive situation like that.

Remember the first C from SUCCEED? Be *Creative*.

There are times when you owe it to yourself—and others—to take control.

And if you can do it without creating a conflict, so much the better.

In life you can either be a passenger or a driver—but only drivers are in control.

Chapter 7
Testing Yourself

It would be all too easy to read this book, try out a few of the ideas and be happy with the benefits they bring.

It would also be possible to try only the easy parts, without applying yourself to the whole program—just try a few things half-heartedly, and then dismiss them if they don't work.

And it would be possible to use the program properly at first, then coast along on the momentum from the initial boost it gives you, and miss out on the long-term benefits.

To avoid pitfalls and to help you cope with the occasional failure, you should test yourself regularly.

Failure?

Yes, there will be times when you feel defeated, when life doesn't work out, when there seems to be no solution.

Testing yourself regularly will help you pinpoint where you went wrong; whether it was your fault or whether someone else let you down.

When things go wrong, ask yourself this: can I turn this negative into a positive? Can I make the best of a bad job? At the very least, can I learn something from this?

Even when things are going well, you should be testing yourself constantly. Here's how it works:

TEST 1

Do you really like yourself?

Can you honestly say, 'I wish I had me as a friend'?

If the answer is anything less than an emphatic 'yes!' go back to the first two chapters of this book and work through them again.

Until you truly like yourself, you can't make any progress.

TEST 2

Do you believe in yourself?

Do you honestly think you've got what it takes? Or have you been harbouring a suspicion that you're not up to it?

Have you really got rid of those negative influences?

Seeing is believing: believing in yourself means seeing yourself in a new light.

Go back to Chapter 3 and check yourself out.

TEST 3

Do you really trust yourself?

Could you allow yourself to give your best shot?
Are you taking those calculated risks that make the difference between surviving and succeeding?

Can you trust yourself to succeed when things start to go wrong?

Trust yourself and you'll never need to trust anyone else.

Chapter 4 will remind you of where you might be going wrong.

TEST 4

Are you being generous enough?
Are you giving yourself enough time to do what you want to do?

Are you giving yourself enough credit for what you achieve?

Are you getting the rewards for the work you are doing?

If you don't get the rewards you deserve, your work will suffer. Then you'll get what you deserve—nothing.

Do yourself a favour—start by re-reading Chapter 5.

TEST 5

Are you challenging yourself?

Are you succeeding more, but deciding not to tempt fate?

Are you trying to do better than your best—or just better than your worst?

Remember, they don't issue score cards on the day you retire. Only you know whether you have succeeded or not.

The toughest rival you'll ever have is yourself—and yours are the only standards worth beating.

Here's another challenge—read Chapter 6 again and see how you measure up.

TEST 6

Now test yourself against the letters from SUCCEED.

Self-confidence

Remember, this is the key to everything else. Are you truly self-confident?

Understanding

Understanding your problems means you can see when they are opportunities in disguise. Do you only see problems instead of looking for solutions?

Creativity

Are you trying to get out of a rut while doing the same old thing you've always done? Are you being creative enough?

Collaboration
Divide the load and multiply the success whenever you can. Are you trying to do it all on your own when you should be collaborating?

Excellence
Enough is never enough if you want success. Are you striving for excellence or making do with second best?

Enjoyment
Business and pleasure are a potently positive combination. Are you enjoying what you do or are you merely trying to enjoy the money you're paid?

Determination
To reach the top you have to keep climbing. Do you look up, see how far it is and lose heart? Do you allow every little setback to knock you off course? Are you as determined as you need to be?

Every time you see a ruler or tape measure, or read about one, or hear one mentioned, remember how important it is to test yourself.

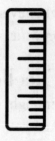

Succeeding With Others

Test yourself by asking someone close to you to analyse your performance using these six tests. You may be missing something.

If someone asks your advice about a problem, try the tests on them. They may discover something to their advantage.

Ask yourself if you're working better with others. If not, ask yourself why not—and read the next chapter.

'Life is the biggest test we'll ever sit. That's the exciting bit about living. There are a million opportunities to grow and learn. Loving, living and learning are why we are here.'

Effie, Greek goddess and author

Power Page 7

E is for Enjoyment

If you work eight hours a day, five days a week, you're spending a third of your waking life at your job.

Add all the time you spend thinking—or even worrying—about work, and that's half of your life.

You are entitled to enjoy life, so you *must* enjoy your work.

Enjoy your job and you'll enjoy the rewards. Wage-slaves *never* feel they're paid enough.

Enjoy each new challenge and be proud of what you achieve. And if things go wrong, anticipate and appreciate the pleasure you will get when you bounce back.

But if your work gives you no pleasure, be prepared to quit. Trust your judgment to know when the job is wrong. Have the self-confidence

to strike out on a new path.
Believe in your ability to succeed.

Better the devil you know? Better no devil at all!

Smart Thinking
Compromise—Not Cop Out

Compromise is not the opposite of conflict—it lies between conflict and unanimous agreement.

But when somebody asks you to compromise, they are often asking you to give way entirely to what they want.

A good compromise is when everyone gets what they need and they get an equal share of what they want.

But one person getting everything they want while another gets nothing is no compromise at all.

Compromise is give *and* take—not give *or* take.

Establish what the other person needs, then find out what they want.

Also ask yourself how important it is for this person to feel they are 'winning' a battle with you. Accepting defeat on a small point may be enough to satisfy them.

Then, using the two C's in SUCCEED, be *Creative* and *Collaborate* on what is good for both of you.

But never compromise on what you need. Give way on that and you're just setting up a conflict further down the road.

Chapter 8
Sharing Success

Throughout this book, I have stressed the importance of 'Me'.

Now that we've got the basics right, it's time to expand that to 'Succeed WITH Me'.

In fact, this is where the whole book has been leading. It's not just a good idea to share your success with others—it's essential.

A problem shared is a problem halved—a success shared is a success doubled.

Learn to share the load with others and you'll want to share the success.

And when others are involved in your success they are less likely to let you fail.

We are talking success networks. A success network may be a loose collaboration of like-minded friends and colleagues or a fairly formal group with set aims—it's up to you.

And while you are at the centre of your success network, others in it may be at the centre of their own success networks, which would certainly include you, but could also include people you've never met. Let me give you an example.

Mary, Ellen, Sandra and Polly are young mothers with preschool age children. They have chosen to stay at home rather than have full-time jobs.

But where they live, suitable part-time work is hard to find.

Nevertheless, Ellen, the thinker of the quartet, decides she wants more than nappies, shopping and kindy. She finds the others agree.

So she gets everyone together and asks, 'What can we do well?'

Mary used to be a salesperson. She has a bubbly, outgoing personality.

Ellen has a business brain, and she and Sandra are excellent cooks.

Polly, who was a high-powered secretary before she had her baby, loves looking after children.

So the four of them set up a boardroom catering firm, using Polly's contacts to find clients.

While Polly minds the children, Ellen and Sandra cook and Mary goes out and sells their service.

That's Ellen's success network. But it's just the start.

Mary, having that outgoing personality, is a member of an amateur theatre group. She and a couple of her theatrical friends branch out into staging children's birthday parties.

Naturally, while Mary and her chums provide the entertainment and organise the games, Ellen and Sandra handle the catering.

That is the beginning of Mary's success network.

Polly doesn't want to be looking after four children *every* day on her own. So she finds two other mums and they work out a roster with two of them looking after six kids while the third does her own thing.

In fact, they club together and buy a computer and printer. Polly teaches the others to use it and they set up a home-based secretarial firm for small businesses in the area.

Naturally, Ellen's catering operation and Mary's party organisers are among their first customers.

That is Polly's success network.

Sandra, inspired by the success of the birthday party scheme, teams up with a couple of artists to branch out into specially decorated and sculpted cakes for all sort of occasions.

That is the start of her success network.

All four stay together to keep the core network going. All four branch off into their separate areas too.

It's a chain reaction. And, as each network grows, the word spreads, the opportunities increase and everyone becomes more successful.

But how would that work in an office? Terri, Doug and Tom are architects in a large city firm. Terri is a computer whiz, Doug is an ideas man and Tom is a 'people person'. One night after work, Terri tells the others that she has an idea. Why don't they pool their resources on all their projects to maximise their chances of success?

They do and it works like a dream. In fact, it works so well that Tom, the 'people person', gets promoted to a bigger section.

Are the others jealous?

Envious, maybe. But they know that Tom realises he owes his success to the network. And they know that as soon as he can manage it, they'll be joining him in that higher section.

Meanwhile, he is feeding the prime projects to Terri and Doug because he knows they will do well, which in turn will reflect well on him.

Terri and Doug come into contact with increasingly powerful people. They learn from them and get a chance to impress them.

Eventually, they get promoted too. And when the network is properly back together, all three are ready to make the next step up. Or even out, since such a powerful team could do well in business for themselves.

That's how working together works. That's how networking works.

So how do you form these networks and how do you make them work? How exactly do you share success?

The principles for sharing success are exactly the same as those for your own success.

Liking Others
and Getting Them to Like You

If you like yourself—and you must like yourself without being smug or patronising—people will be drawn to you. If you look for the qualities in others that you like in yourself (or wish you had) you will have the basis for strong relationships.

Don't waste your time and energy with people you don't like.

When you have given time to yourself and your friends you will have no time for enemies.

Believing in Others and
Getting Them to Believe in You

Once you've made the leap in thinking that allows you to believe in yourself, it isn't so hard to believe in others.

Look for qualities you feel *you* have, then for those you wish you had.

Allow those you work with to express their opinions and use their ideas whenever you can. And always give them credit.

When the best idea isn't yours, the bright idea is to back it to the hilt.

Life is too short for ego battles. Stifling someone else's ambition and creativity is the surest way to make a dangerous enemy of a good friend.

Don't worry about being overshadowed by others who strive for success. Ambitious and creative people will be drawn to you when you show that you are prepared to believe in them.

And it will soon be obvious who is at the centre of this success network. You!

Trusting Others and Getting Them to Trust You

If you like someone and believe in them, you *must* trust them.

If you don't trust others, they are unlikely to trust you.

Everybody deserves one chance. Give it freely and offer as much help as you can.

Most of the people you like and believe in will come good, valuing the trust you've placed in them.

But be careful!

Trusting the wrong people devalues the trust you place in others.

And it puts valuable friendships under too much strain.

People will instinctively trust you when they see that you are selective about whom you trust.

Never confuse trust with blind faith—one is for people with vision.

Being Generous with Others

All the principles of being generous with yourself apply here, too.

Be generous with your time. Spend time helping people with their problems and enjoying their successes. This applies especially to your family and friends. If, in becoming a success, you become a stranger to those who love you, you haven't succeeded at all.

Be generous with your praise, your trust and your advice. These are all more important than being generous with money or material rewards. But when rewards are in order, be generous with them.

Your generosity with others is an expression of your belief in yourself.

Challenging Others

When you have started on the road to success, the people who are drawn to you will become part of your success network.

They will look to you for inspiration and leadership. But that needn't mean that you will be telling them what to do. You will be challenging them to achieve what they want. You will be the one saying, 'What a great idea. I think you can do it. Don't let yourself down by not trying.'

People will come to you for advice and help, but the most important thing you can say is, 'You can do it.'

Similarly, these people will be the ones who urge you to 'Do it'. And they will be there to help you when you need it.

Mountain tops are very lonely places—don't climb every mountain on your own.

Testing Each Other

The previous chapter dealt with how to test yourself to see if you are making the most of your efforts to succeed. It also described how to apply those tests to others.

Once you have established a success network of friends and colleagues, you can apply some of those tests to the network.

If you prefer to work as a loose collaboration of friends, colleagues and family, ask yourself occasionally if you are getting as much from the network as it is getting from you.

Identify weak links and either strengthen them or replace them. As you do so, the network will bind more closely around you.

You may, however, want to establish the core of your network as a more defined group. Encourage those you wish to include to read this book, or explain the basic principles to them. Then occasionally have a group discussion to test yourselves as a network. You should be asking yourselves:

- Do we as individuals like this group and have confidence in it and the people in it?
- Do we believe in this group and the individuals in it?
- Do we trust this group and the individuals in it?

Answering these kinds of questions requires a special kind of honesty, but the network will be stronger at the end of it.

Some members may be sceptical, but you can win them over by proving yourself right.

As with the whole of 'Succeed With Me', there are no easy answers, just a clear way forward.

And remember this:

Every step in an uphill struggle takes you higher.

Every time you see a handshake, or read about one, or hear one mentioned, remember how important it is to share your success.

'How fortunate we are in this magnificent country to have the land as our livelihood and friends as companions, and faith and love as our tools. We must believe in ourselves, never accept mediocrity, and in reaching out to each other, so we must reach upwards to the stars. For are we not angels in training? All we have to do is spread our wings and learn to fly.'

Terry Underwood, author

Power Page 8

D is for Determination

The last letter of SUCCEED gives us the last word on the subject of success.

Down the ages people have succeeded without education, money or even talent—provided they had determination. Few have succeeded without it.

Nothing worthwhile is easy. If success was as simple as saying, 'Aren't I clever?', everybody would be millionaires.

You have to work at it. You have to put more effort into everything you do—including your relationships.

You have to remember to be positive, whatever happens.

You must *never* give up. When life kicks you in the teeth, pick yourself up and start again.

Determination makes dreams come true.

You will succeed because you can succeed.

Take the first step. Shoulder that load. Look up. Keep going.

Say to yourself, 'Succeed With Me!' And you will.

Smart Thinking

Give Yourself a Chance

I have told you about aiming high; about setting goals and striving for them; about always trying to be the best you can be.

These are all important, but you have to be realistic. Only set yourself achievable goals.

Aim for results that you can reasonably hope to get.

Athletes who break world records get there by constantly surpassing their own personal bests.

It's all done step by step and sometimes it takes years.

It's okay to want a five million dollar mansion, but start by aiming for an extra bedroom or a beach house.

Aiming too high too soon is almost as bad as aiming too low. You are setting yourself up for failure and disappointment.

Enjoy each achievement for what it is while striving for a little more.

Learn to appreciate what you have achieved, congratulate yourself, share your success—then move on.

Live each day for today *and* tomorrow.

Learn from the past, savour the present, anticipate the future.

Every small step gives you the thrill of anticipation as a wish becomes a hope, then a possibility, then a probability.

If you make all your little dreams come true, then the big ones will come true too.

And if things go wrong and you fail—even if it's through no fault of your own—you will have all those little successes behind you to build on.

No matter how far you've travelled, you still go forward step by step.

Remember: by the time you see a shooting star, it's already on its way down.

There is no such thing as overnight success— just quiet achievers who got where they wanted before anyone noticed.

Once you start to be that kind of success, it's very hard to stop.

'Sometimes the best way to find the source of a problem is to look in a mirror.'
Scott Gibbons, real estate agent

Suggested Inspirational Reading

Coustas, Mary, *Effie's Guide to Being Upyourself*, Hodder Headline, 2003

Hamilton, Maggie, *Coming Home: Rediscovering our Sacred Selves*, Penguin Books, 2002

Jackson, Carole, *Colour Me Beautiful*, Little Hills Press, 1990

Kolm, John and Ring, Peter, *Crocodile Charlie and the Holy Grail*, Penguin Books, 2003

McNally, Patrick, *Free Your Mind and Change Your Life*, New Holland, 2003

Morton, Cynthia J, *Helping Hand with Life Hodder Headline*, 2002

Rochester, AJ, *Confessions of a Reformed Dieter*, Random House, 2003

Sher, Barbara, *I Could Do Anything, If Only I Knew What It Was*, Hodder Headline, 1995

Underwood, Terry, *In the Middle of Nowhere*, Random House, 1999

Williams, Sue, *Mean Streets, Kind Heart: the Father Chris Riley Story*, HarperCollins, 2003

You can visit Selwa's website at:
www.selwaanthony.com.au.

Succeed With Me

'Don't give up, never *give up!'*
Toni Lamond, actress/author